Paleo Crock Pot Recipes

70 Paleo Slow Cooker Recipes

By: Kevin L. Kerr

2 Paleo Crock Pot Recipes

Table of Contents

Herbal Chicken-Kale Soup

Ingredients:

- 1 1/2 tsp of fresh parsley

- 4 cups of fresh kale (chopped)

- 1 cup of baby carrots (shredded)

- 4 garlic cloves (finely diced)

- 1/2 cup of white onion (finely diced)

- 3-4 cups of chicken broth (homemade)

- 6 chicken thighs (organic, deboned and skinless)

- Salt and pepper to taste

Instructions:

Wash the chicken thighs and put them into the slow cooker. Add the onion and garlic. Next, pour in the chicken broth.

Cover and cook for 6 hours on low. Once chicken is tender after about five hours use a fork or other utensil to separate it. Add the kale, parsley, salt, pepper, and carrots.

Cook for another hour and let it cool. Serve and enjoy!

Cashew-Masala Chicken Pizza

Ingredients:

For the Pizza Toppings:

- 1/2 cup of fresh cilantro (finely chopped)
- 1 1/2 lbs. of chicken thighs (organic, deboned and skinless)
- 1 cup of smoked Gouda cheese (crumbled)
- 1/2 small yellow onion (minced)
- A pinch of cayenne pepper
- 2 cups of tomato sauce
- 1 tsp of salt
- 2 tbsp. of garam masala powder
- 1/2 tsp of paprika
- 1 tsp of ginger (dried)

For the Crust:

- 1 tsp of apple cider vinegar
- 1 cup whole raw cashews (fresh)
- 3 tbsps. of cold water

- 1/2 cup of coconut flour/cream
- 3/4 cup of almond milk
- 3 tbsps. of extra virgin olive oil
- 5 beaten eggs (large)
- 1 1/2 teaspoon of curry powder
- 1 1/2 tsp of baking mix soda
- 1/2 tsp of salt

Instructions:

Combine the cayenne pepper, tomato sauce, salt, onions, paprika, 1/4 cup of water and garam masala powder. Mix together and put it in the slow cooker. Put the organic chicken in your crock pot and cook for 6 hours on low.

30 minutes before the set time, preheat the oven to 350 degrees Fahrenheit.

Use a blender or food processor and blend the cashews until finely grinded and smooth in texture.

Add the curry powder, salt, baking soda, coconut flour and almond flour. Blend together until totally mixed. Next, add in the water, olive oil, vinegar, apple cider, milk, and eggs. Process and blend for 1 minute. It will form a smooth dough. Set aside.

On a piece parchment paper, drizzle some of the almond flour and put the dough onto it. Sprinkle some flour over the dough ball and place another sheet of parchment paper on top of it.

Using bare hands form the dough into pieces of round pizza-like crust for about ¼″ thick.

Remove the parchment paper from the top. Using a round non-stick baking pan, bake for 10-12 minutes or until the crust turns golden brown.

Meanwhile, chop the chicken into pieces. Turn the slow cooker off and add the cashew mixture. Add the chicken after your cut it up and stir well.

Remove the pizza crust from the oven and scoop some of the chicken and sauce over the crust (grease the crust with olive oil) Top over some cheese and bake it for 15 minutes or until cheese is melted.

Serve with fresh cilantro and enjoy!

<u>Spicy Beef Fajitas</u>

Ingredients:

- 1 red and 1 green of bell peppers (seeded and julienned)

- 2 1/2 lbs of beef sirloin (grass-fed) you can use any soft or lean meat of beef)

- 2 jalapeños of 1 large of poblano pepper (seeded and julienned)

- 1 onion (red, large and diced)

For the Dry Spice Rub:

- 1/2 tsp of cayenne pepper and 1/4 extra

- 1 teaspoon of salt

- 1/4 tsp of onion powder

- 1/2 tsp of fresh ground black pepper

- 1/4 tsp of garlic powder

- 2 tsps. of chili paste or powder

- 1 tsp of cumin

For the Garnish and Serving:

- Cherry tomatoes, slices of limes, fresh cilantro sprigs, romaine lettuce or mixed vegetables.

Instructions:

Mix all the ingredients for the dry spice rub into a small bowl, stir well to mix together. Rub the mixed spices on all sides of the beef meat. Place the meat onto the slow cooker.

Put the peppers and onion on top and cover. Simmer and cook for 10 hours on low.

Few minutes before the set time, add in the jalapeños and cook until beef is tender.

Top it with avocado and steamed cauliflower. Serve and enjoy!

Broccauliflower Meatball Soup

Ingredients:

- 1 parsnip (finely sliced)
- 4 tbsp of olive oil
- 1 zucchini (finely chopped)
- 1 yellow onion (finely chopped)
- 3 stalks of celery (finely chopped)
- 1 cup of broccoli florets
- 1 cup of cauliflower florets
- 3 cloves of minced garlic
- 3 cups of baby spinach
- 1 large fresh tomato (cubed)
- 1/4 cup of almond meal
- 32 ounces of beef broth
- 1 pound of grass-fed ground beef
- 1/2 tsp of garlic powder
- 1 tsp of oregano powder
- 2 tbsp of fresh basil leaves

- 2 eggs (medium, beaten)

- 1 tsp of black pepper

Instructions:

In a slow cooker pot pour 2-3 tbsps. olive oil and heat. Add the celery, onion and cook for 10 minutes then mix in the fresh garlic. As the basil, pinch of salt, cubed tomato, oregano, all other vegetables and beef broth. Bring to boil and simmer for 15 minutes.

While waiting, prepare the mixture for the meatballs. Get a small bowl; mix the beef, garlic powder and beaten eggs, 1 teaspoon of oregano, pepper and almond meal. Wash your hand and mix the ingredients until thick and firm. Roll beef mixture to meat balls. Add them to the slow cooker.

Add the remaining of the basil and spinach and cover.

Cook on low for 4 hours or until meatballs are fully cooked and tender.

Serve hot over a bowl of rice!

Coco Spicy Shrimp Soup

Ingredients:

- A pinch of salt and pepper
- 2 lbs. of medium raw shrimp (peeled and deveined)
- 1 lime (juiced)
- 3 tbsps. of coconut oil
- 1 tbsp. of chili garlic sauce (or you can use sriracha)
- 1 medium red onion, finely chopped
- 1 can of coconut milk or cream
- 3 cloves of garlic (smashed)
- 1 can of diced tomatoes (drained)
- 2 jalapeños (sliced)
- 1/4 cup of fresh chopped cilantro

Instructions:

Heat oil in a large skillet over medium heat, then first to sauté' is the onion and pepper for 3 minutes until aromatic. Add the tomatoes, garlic, and shrimp. Pour in the sautéed seasonings into the slow cooker. Add the shrimp, coconut milk, jalapeño and chili sauce.

Cover and cook for 1 hour low.

Sprinkle the lime juice, season with the salt and pepper.

Serve with avocado and cilantro as toppings or any of your favorites.

Serve and enjoy!

Chili Turkey And Sweet Potato

Ingredients:

- 1 can of tomato paste (6 oz can)
- 1 lb of ground turkey (organic)
- 1 can of whole tomatoes (28 oz)
- 1 white onion (chopped finely)
- 2 lbs of sweet potato
- 2 cloves of minced garlic
- 1 tbsp of chili paste or chili powder
- 1 tsp of ground cumin
- 2 tsp of salt
- 1/2 tsp of dried oregano
- 1 tbsp of ancho chili powder

Toppings:

- Cheese, lime, sour cream, avocado or cilantro

Instructions:

Put the turkey meat (organic), garlic, onions, salt and spices in the slow cooker. Mix together .Wash the sweet potatoes and peel them. Cut it into quarters. Put them all in the slow cooker. Blend the whole tomatoes and tomato paste in a processor. Blend until roughly chunky mixture forms. Pour into crock pot.

Cover and cook on low for 10 hours until turkey meat are tender and potatoes are done.

Add salt to taste.

Serve with the desired toppings!

Yummy Chorizo Yams

Ingredients:

- 1/4 tsp of freshly ground pepper
- 1/2 tsp of salt
- 3 cloves of minced garlic
- 1/2 tsp of diced yellow onion
- 3 yams (peeled & diced)
- 1 lb of chorizo (skinless)
- 2 tbsp of butter (grass-fed)

***cilantro sprigs for garnish

Instructions:

Put the yams into the crock pot.

In a medium skillet, heat the butter in medium-low temp. Sauté onions and garlic for 1 minute or until you smell the aroma of the onions. Mix the chorizo and sauté until brown. Add everything into the cooker. Add salt and pepper to season it.

Cook on low for 6 hours.

Separate the yams into a bowl and mash it with fork.

Serve and garnish with cilantro!

Spicy Chicken With Pineapple Slaw

Ingredients:

- 4 pounds of pork roast (grass-fed)

- 1 tsp of liquid smoke (Natural liquid)

- 1 tbsp of black pepper

- 2 cups of chicken stock (home-made)

- 1 tsp of salt

- 1/4 cup of balsamic vinegar

- 1 tsp of chipotle chile powder

For the pineapple slaw:

- Salt and pepper to taste

- 4 cups of coleslaw (1/2 cup of red cabbage, 1/4 cup of green cabbage, 2 baby carrots)

- 2 cups of fresh pineapple

- 1 1/2 tbsp of apple cider vinegar

Instructions:

Put all the ingredients in a bowl.

Spice the meat with the mixture. Put it into the slow cooker.

Add the liquid smoke; pour in the stock and the balsamic. Stir and cover.

Cook for 8 hours on low.

Shred the meat using a fork. Put it in a bowl and serve. Pour with some juices from the crock pot.

Serve with desired toppings!

Serve with the pineapple slaw and enjoy!

Lamb Meat With Sweet Potato Noodle Soup

Ingredients:

- Salt and pepper
- cracked-whole pepper
- 2 tbsp of olive oil
- 2 tbsp of butter or lard (or any healthy fats)
- 1/2 thigh of lamb/ or you may use leg of the lamb
- 2 peeled sweet potatoes
- 1/2 cup of water or better to use beef stock (home-made)
- Juice and zest of 1 lime
- 3 stalks of rosemary
- 4 garlic cloves (minced)
- 3 stalks of celery (finely chopped)

***flat-leaf parsley (garnish)

Instructions:

Wash, rinse and pat dry the lamb meat. Be sure to cut it into half so it will fit into the crock pot. Drizzle salt and pepper to desired seasoning.

In a food processor, put the rosemary leaves with lemon zest and garlic. Blend until completely mixed. Pour some of the olive oil and blend again for another minute.

Spread the mixture into the lamb meat and put it in the fridge for 2 hours or much better if overnight.

Pour water or stock then squeeze the zested lemon.

Cook for 8 hours or until lamb meat is fully tender and done. Allow it to cool.

In preparing for the noodle soup; peel and cut the potatoes 1/3 each (lengthwise). Get a spiral peeler or cutter to create a noodle strand.

In a small skillet, heat the butter and put strand of noodles. Season the noodles with salt and pepper. Cook for at least 5-8 minutes until sweet potatoes are tender.

Put it in a serving bowl, top with lamb meat, pour in the soup and serve!

Garnish with cilantro. Enjoy!

Pork Shanks and Tomatoes

Ingredients:

- ¾ cups of homemade chicken stock
- 1 tbsp of ghee, lard or coconut oil
- 14 oz chopped tomatoes
- 3 lbs of bone-in pork shanks (grass-fed)
- 2 small lemons (zested and juiced)
- 3 cups of onion (1 large red onion)
- 1 tsp of salt
- ½ tsp of pepper
- 2 cups of baby carrots (diced)
- 2 tbsp of freshly chopped basil
- 3 cups of whole mushroom (chopped)
- 1 tbsp of fresh oregano (minced)
- 3 cloves of garlic (minced)
- 2 tbsp of fresh thyme

Instructions:

Wash the shanks thoroughly and dry it using some towels or paper towels.

In a large sauce pan, add ½ tbsp of lard (or any healthy fats) over medium-high heat. Sear the pork shanks each side for about 7-8 minutes. Leave it on the side.

In the same pan, pour in the remaining fats, add the garlic carrots and onion and cook for 2-3 minutes, pour this mixture into the slow cooker and then add the pork shanks.

Heat the skillet and drizzle the lemon juice to deglaze the pan. Pour the drippings in the crock pot as the sauce of your meal. Mix in the lemon zest, mushrooms, basil, salt, oregano and thyme.

Add the stock and the tomatoes and cover.

Cook on low for 6 hours.

Remove the shanks and set aside. Let it warm.

Pour the liquid from the crock pot to a blender or food processor. Add half of the vegetables, and blend. Puree until smooth. Adjust the seasonings if necessary.

Pour the puree into the slow cooker, stir and add the pork shanks.

Cover and cook on low for another 30 minutes. Serve and enjoy!

Chicken Stew With Squash And Herbs

Ingredients:

- A handful of fresh parsley (for garnish and for seasoning)
- 4 lbs of chicken thighs (organic, deboned and skinless)
- ¼ tsp of pepper and ¼ tsp of salt
- 2 cups of butternut squash (1/2 of the medium, peeled and chopped)
- ¼ tsp of thyme
- 1 large carrot (1/2 cup)
- 1 tsp of herbs de Provence
- 2 stalks of celery (roughly chopped)
- 2 bay leaves
- ½ cup of chopped red onion
- ½ cup of dry white wine
- 4 garlic cloves (minced)
- 1 can of diced tomatoes (w/ juice)
- ½ cup of chicken broth (home-made)

Instructions:

Wash and peel the squash. Cut it in half and then cut it into chunks or bite-size cubes.

Same with carrots wash and chop to bite size.

Put all the vegetables into the slow cooker. Add the seasonings and all ingredients. Mix all using a wooden ladle.

Add the chicken thighs and cover. Cover and cook for 5-6 hours and low.

Remove the bay leaves and throw it. Stir occasionally. Shred the chicken thigh. Meat should fall apart from its bone. Taste and put some salt and pepper if need.

Top it with parsley and enjoy!

Pork Goodness In Saffron Tea

Ingredients:

- ½ tsp of Saffron

- 4 lbs of pork spare ribs (grass-fed) (about 4 large cuts)

- 1 tbsp of paprika

- ¼ cup of hot water

- 1 tsp of coriander, powdered

- 1 ½ tsp of ground cumin

- 1 tsp of fresh oregano leaves

- 1 tsp of red pepper flakes of red chili sauce

- 1 Tablespoons of Fresh Chive

- 1 Tablespoon of Fresh Parsley

- 1 large onion (quartered)

- 4 minced garlic cloves

- 2 tbsp of ghee, coconut oil or lard

- 1 can of diced tomato (28 oz can)

- 2 tsp of salt (or have some extra)

For the Sauce:

- 1 tbsp of arrowroot starch
- ¼ cup of full-fat coconut milk
- 2 tbsp of healthy fat
- 1 cup broth (home-made)

Instructions:

In a teacup, put the saffron and pour hot water. Leave it on the side.

Combine the pepper flakes, paprika, coriander, oregano and cumin.

In a medium skillet, add ghee or cooking fat and sear the spare ribs into golden brown. Sear each side for 8 minutes or until brown.

Transfer the spare ribs into the slow cooker.

Combine the garlic, onion and the spiced mixture on the skillet and cook for 5 minutes stirring constantly. Pour a little amount of cooking fat or liquid from the tomatoes if skillet is getting dried.

Put all the ingredients from skillet into crock pot. Add the tomatoes and saffron tea, salt, parsley and chives.

Cover and cook on low for 8 hours.

In cooking the sauce:

Scoop a cup of broth from the slow cooker. Add ghee, broth and coconut milk in the saucepan. Heat for 5 minutes or until liquid mixture was reduced. Drizzle the arrowroot and stir until dissolved.

Spiced Pulled Pork In Tomatoes

Ingredients:

- 2 cloves of garlic, finely chopped
- 1 small yellow onion (Sliced thinly)
- 1-2 lbs of pork shoulder
- 2 slices of beef or pork bacon (fat-free)
- 1/4 cup of chicken broth (homemade)
- Salt and pepper
- 1/4 tsp of cinnamon
- 1/2 Tbsp of apple cider vinegar
- 1-1/4 tsp of chili powder
- 1 medium date (pitted and coarsely chopped)
- 2 tsp of cumin
- 2 Tbsp of tomato sauce or tomato paste

Instructions:

In a large pan, heat oil and add the bacon. Cook over medium-high heat. Mix the garlic and onion. Stir and cook together for about 5 minutes. Set heat to low.

Check if bacon is already fully cooked; if so add the tomato paste and remove from heat. Pour in the cider vinegar and dates. Transfer into slow cooker.

Wash and rinse the pork shoulder. Season it salt and pepper. In the same pan, sear the meat and put some oil. Brown it for 6 minutes each side. add into the slow cooker.

In a small bowl, combine dry ingredients, salt, chili powder, cumin and cinnamon. Mix all together and pour it in the slow cooker.

Cover and cook on low for 8 hours. Shred the pork meat using fork.

Serve with mixed vegetables or toppings of your choice!

You can garnish it with avocado and cilantro.

Carne Asada In Spicy Lettuce Wraps

Ingredients:

- 2 lbs steak, grass-fed (I used to have the boneless sirloin but any tough parts are fine to use)

- Carne Asada

- 2 tbsp of minced garlic

- 1 medium yellow onion (finely chopped)

- 1 4oz- can of fire roasted diced green chilies (mine is at Trader Joes)

- 2-3 medium-sizes of tomatoes (chopped)

- 2 small limes, juiced

- 1/3 cup of beef broth (homemade)

- 1 tbsp of cumin

- 2 tbsp of chili powder

- Salt to taste

- 1/2 tsp cayenne pepper

- Pepper, to taste

- Garlic powder

***you may use these for garnish and toppings (cilantro, limes, hot sauce, roasted salsa, romaine lettuce, or any lettuce leaves, slice of avocados, salsa)

Instructions:

Wash and rinse the steak meat and use paper towels to pat the meat dry.

Spread to season the meat with salt, powdered garlic and pepper on both side. Leave it for a while.

Chop the tomatoes and onions in quarters.

Pour into the slow cooker with the beef broth.

Add the steak and submerge it into the broth. Add garlic, tomatoes, onions, garlic and chilies.

Drizzle it with lime juice all over the meat mixture.

Add the cayenne, cumin and chili powder.

Gently toss and stir to fold ingredients together.

Cover and cook for 8 hours on low.

Shred the steak meat using two forks.

Serve over a lettuce-cup leaf with your choice of toppings!

Classic Whole Roast Chicken

Ingredients:

- 2 tsp of salt

- 1 whole, organic or nature-farmed chicken

- 1/2 tsp of organic black pepper (ground)

- 1 tsp of organic white pepper

- 2 tsp of organic paprika

- 1 tsp of organic cayenne pepper

- 3 sprigs of fresh rosemary (or 1 tsp of dried rosemary)

- 1/2 tsp of organic garlic powder

- 3 medium-sized potatoes (cubed)

- 1 large onion, loosely chopped

Instructions:

In a large bowl, combine all dry spices. Mix together and set aside. a small bowl and set aside.

Wash and pat dry the chicken using a cloth or a paper towel.

Arrange the onions on the bottom of the crock pot (the reason behind is to avoid the skins of the meat sticking onto the crock pot)

Add potatoes and chicken.

Before placing the chicken, make sure to spice rub it with the spice mixtures.

Cover and cook for 6 hours on low.

Serve when chicken is thoroughly cooked.

Enjoy this delectable dish!

Basil Tomato Soup

Ingredients:

- food processor
- 2 cups of yellow onion (chopped)
- 2 lbs of tomatoes (peeled & chopped) or 1 can of 28-oz diced tomato
- ¼ tsp of salt
- 1/8 tsp of pepper
- 1/8 tsp of red pepper flakes or chili flakes
- 1 tbsp of 2 cloves garlic
- ½ tsp of dried basil
- ¼ tsp of smoked paprika
- 1 cup of chicken broth (homemade)
- 1 tbsp of raw honey

bay leaves, Greek yogurt and fresh basil for serving

Instructions:

Chop onion coarsely and put it in a pan. Heat the pan with olive oil on medium to low heat.

Season it with salt and pepper. Stir continuously and let it cook for 6 minutes.

Add the tomato and tomato juice to the pan.

Add the pepper flakes and smoked paprika (you can adjust the spiciness of the soup to the level of hotness you can take). Add the remaining of the spices, last is the honey. Stir and mix until fully incorporated.

Taste then if it's already good for you, add it to the crock pot. Pour in the chicken broth and cover. Cook for 6 hours on low. Let It warm.

Remove the bay leaves. Pour the soup into the blender or food processor until to the level of smoothness you want when eating soup. You may want to crunch some of the chunks of the tomatoes!

Serve it with Greek yogurt and garnish with basil. Top with cheese or any side dish you want to combine. It's Gouda!

Chicken Wings With Veggie Salad

Ingredients:

- Mixed veggie salad

- Spices (salt and pepper)

- Chicken Wings about 3-4 pieces (organic)

Instructions:

Put the chicken wings into the crock pot. Sprinkle the spices over the chicken and cover. Cook on 4 hours low.

With the set time to cook, prepare the veggie salad.

Serve on a plate with the salad.

Broiled Pork Chops With Veggies On Side

Ingredients:

- 3-slices of pork chops (grass–fed)

- Spices like salt, pepper and some herbs

- Mixed vegetables

- Olive oil

- Cooking spray

Instructions:

Wash the pork chops and dry it using paper towels.

Grease the crock pot with the cooking spray. Arrange the pork chops evenly in the slow cooker.

Set stove to broil, or cook on low for 4 hours until meat is tender and ready to serve.

In a frying pan, put the remaining of the olive oil and mix the veggies. Season it with salt and pepper.

Serve the pork chops in a plate and scoop the veggies on the side!

This is one of my favorite lunch meals. I hope you too!

Fried Beef in Onions and Bell Peppers

Ingredients:

- Ground beef (grass-fed)
- Red and Green Bell Peppers
- Salt
- Pepper
- Coconut oil

Instructions:

Slice the onions in quarters.

Add all the ingredients onto the slow cooker, except for the bell peppers

Add the ground beef, cover and cook for 2 hours low.

Fry the bell peppers and add it onto the beef.

Serve with slices of fresh bell peppers.

Paleo Short Ribs In Apple & Pomegranate

You will need:

- 1 ½ - 3 lbs of boneless short ribs (grass-fed pork)

- Salt and pepper to season the pork

- ½ tsp of nutmeg

- ½ tsp of cumin

- 2 tbsp of coconut sap (crystals)

- 1-2 red onions (medium, sliced thinly)

- 1-2 bottles (8 oz) of pomegranate juice (pure)

- 1-2 apples (medium, pink lady, peeled, sliced very thin)

How to cook it:

Mix the sliced onion and apple in the slow cooker.

Add pomegranate juice, 1 tbsp of coconut sap and all other spices. Toss and mix well.

Season the short pork ribs with salt, pepper and the remaining 1 tbsp of coconut sap crystal.

Place the ribs on top of the onion – pomegranate mixture into the slow cooker. Keep it covered while cooking.

Cook it for 4-5 hrs on low.

Sear the ribs in a cast iron skillet just enough to turn it to lightly brown.

Garnish and serve!

Goat Masala Curry

Ingredients:

- 2 medium red-onions (chopped)
- 2 lbs of goat meat (grass-fed)
- 4 cloves of garlic-minced
- 2 inch ginger-minced
- 1 tbsp of organic grass-fed ghee
- 1 bay leaf
- 2 ½ cardamom pods
- 3 Cloves (whole)
- 1 tsp of cumin-powder
- 1 tbsp of coriander-powder
- 2 tsp of salt- to adjust
- 1 tsp of turmeric-powder
- 1 tsp of Chili powder
- 1 tsp of paprika
- 2 serrano pepper-minced

Additional ingredients to add in latter:

- 1 tsp of garam masala

- 1 can of diced tomato – organic

- 1 cup of water

Instructions:

In a blender, grind the cloves and cardamom.

Combine all ingredients into the crock pot except for garam masala, water and tomatoes. Using a ladle spoon, gently toss to mix the ingredients. Turn on crock pot and set to high, cook for 4 hours. Stir occasionally.

After the set time, the remaining ingredients and cook for another hour. Check meat until desired doneness.

Serve while it's hot and enjoy the curry goodie!

Cantonese Ham Soup With Lotus Root

Ingredients:

- 10 red date-berries

- 10 cups of water

- 1 bone-ham with meat (or spare pork ribs) – organic

- 2 lotus-roots (peeled and cut)

Instructions:

Cut or slice the peeled lotus roots lengthwise or to any desired cut. Soak them into a bowl of warm water for 3 minutes. Wash and rinse. Put it onto the slow cooker.

Combine all the ingredients to the slow cooker and cover.

Cook it for 6 hours on low.

Serve the soup while it's hot to enjoy!

You can refrigerate the leftover and it is still good the next day.

Grilled Turkey Patties In Sesame Buns

Ingredients:

- 4 medium buns (sesame seed buns, toasted) (2 ounce)

- 1 lb of ground meat turkey (nature farmed turkeys)

- ¼ cups of barbecue sauce

- 1 clove of garlic (minced)

- ¼ tsp of ground cumin

- ½ teaspoon of powdered paprika

- A dash of kosher salt

- 4 medium sweet onions (grilled)

- ¼ tsp of ground-fresh black pepper

Instructions:

Combine the cumin, turkey meat, paprika and garlic in a medium bowl. Mix together until meat is fully seasoned.

Wash your hands. On a flat platform or clean flat surface in your working kitchen, from turkey meat into 6 patties (2" thick). Season the patties with salt and pepper. Arrange it in the crock pot, cover and cook on high for 2 hours. Remove patties and let cool.

Use a non-stick grilling pan, slightly greased with oil or cooking spray, arrange the patties and grill over medium-high. Turn once in a while sides of patties to make sure that it will be fully cooked and grilled. You can also grill for 2-3 minutes each side (since it's already pre-cooked)

Serve it with the sesame buns and make your own toppings for your burger!

Chicken Salsa De Tortilla

Ingredients:

- 1 cup of chicken broth (homemade)
- 1 cup of cheddar cheese (around 4 oz) (crumbled)
- Cooking spray
- 15 small tortillas (cut into 1") strips
- 1 cup of black beans (drained and rinsed) (around 15 oz)
- 1 cup of onion (finely chopped)
- 1 can of salsa de chile fresco (around 7 ¾ oz)
- 2 cups of chopped chicken breast (organic)
- 5 cloves of garlic (minced)

Instructions:

Turn on the oven to 450°.

Use cooking spray to coat the pan. Cook onion and garlic medium-high heat or until you smell the aroma. Add the chicken and stir for 1 minute. Remove from the pan and put it in a bowl then put the beans.

Pour on the chicken broth and salsa in to the slow cooker. Keep it covered and cook for about 4 hours on low and leave it for a while.

In a glass baking dish (11 x 7 inch) coated with cooking spray, arrange half of the tortilla strips onto the bottom. Spread a layer of chicken mixture over the tortillas. Layer the half of the remaining tortillas on top of the mixture. Repeat the procedures with the remaining of the ingredients. Sprinkle the crumbled cheese on top.

Bake and cook for 10 minutes until cheese is melted. Let it cool for 5 minutes and serve.

Pork Medallion In Red Curry

You will need:

- 2 lbs of pork tenderloin (grass-fed, sliced into ½" round)

- 2 tbsp of red curry powder or paste

- ½-1 can of coconut milk.

- 1 medium white or yellow onion

Instructions:

Pour coconut milk into the crock pot and mix the curry paste. Stir well to dissolve the curry.

Put pork in the mixture as flat as possible so as to coat evenly.

Sprinkle the sliced onions on top of the pork.

Cover and cook on low for 6 hours.

Sprinkle a dash of salt and pepper to taste.

Chicken Roll with Asparagus & Prosciutto

You will need:

- 4 chicken breast (medium, boneless)

- 6-8 pieces prosciutto (or any flavor of ham)

- 1 Handful of asparagus

- 6-8 Cloves of garlic

- A pinch of salt and pepper to taste

Instructions:

You need to fillet the chicken breast in half.

Flatten the fillet using a roll-up wood. Sprinkle salt and pepper. Carefully smash up the chicken until its ready to be rolled-up.

Cut asparagus stalk about halfway to include on the roll.

Put (3) stalks of asparagus and garlic, finely sliced, into the chicken roll

Roll one slice of ham or Prosciutto or ham surrounding the chicken roll and that's it!

Use a wooden toothpick to secure the roll.

Carefully arrange the chicken rolls into the crock pot and cook it in 4 hrs on low.

What a delicious meal to serve!

Chili Shredded Beef

Ingredients:

- 3 lbs of sirloin steak- grass-fed
- 2 large yellow onions-sliced
- ½ cups of beef broth-homemade
- 1 tsp of salt
- ½ tsp of paprika
- ½ tsp of ground black pepper
- ½ tsp of garlic-powdered
- ¼ tsp of chili paste or chili powder
- ¼ teaspoon of white pepper

Instructions:

Wash the steak meat and add into slow cooker. Pour into the broth and onions on top. Add all the spices and mix together.

Cover and let it cook for 8 hours low.

Shred the meat using two forks.

Serve it over a bowl of rice. Enjoy!

Asian Sesame Honey Beef

Ingredients:

- 1 lime –juiced
- 6 lbs of nature-pastured beef (short ribs or spare ribs)
- 3 tbsp of white wine vinegar
- 3 tbsp of coconut aminos
- 1 tbsp of sesame oil
- 1 tbsp of raw-honey
- 1 tsp of hot sauce (any brand)
- 2 tsp of grated-fresh ginger
- 2 tsp of sesame seeds
- Pepper
- Salt

Instructions:

Wash and rinse the spare ribs. Put it in a shallow pan or dish.

Mix all ingredients in a bowl and stir until mixture is soft and thick.

Put the chopped ribs into the marinade bowl, cover and let it set in the fridge overnight.

Put the marinated spare ribs into the slow cooker. Scrape the bowl to scoop all the sauce and include it in the crock pot.

Cover on with the lid and cook for 8 hours on low or until meat falls off its bone.

Serve!

Sugar-Dessert Crock Pot Stuffed Apples

Ingredients:

- ½ cup of coconut cream or coconut butter-homemade
- 4 medium-green apples, cored
- ¼ cup of nut butter- unsweetened
- 2 tbsp of cinnamon
- A pinch of nutmeg and salt
- 4 tbsp of shredded –coconut
- 1 cup of water

Instructions:

Mix the nut butter and coconut butter, along with the salt and nutmeg in a bowl. Mix along to incorporate.

Arrange the apples into the crock pot and pour 1 cup of water.

Spoon a mixture of butter onto each of the apple top.

Sprinkle the cinnamon powder on top of the apple and put some shredded coconut.

Cover with lid on and cook for 3 hours low.

Serve with ice cream!

Lentil Soup With Pitas

Ingredients:

- 6 whole-grain pitas (cut in half and toasted)
- 1 tbsp of olive oil
- 3 tbsp of fresh lemon juice
- 1 tbsp of olive oil
- 1 cup of lentils (dried)
- stalk of celery (chopped)
- 1 ½ sliced onion
- 2 baby carrots (chopped)
- 6 cups of water
- 2 cloves of garlic (minced)
- ½ tsp of salt
- 2 tsp of oregano (dried)
- ¼ tsp of pepper

Instructions:

Put all the ingredients onto the cooker. Cook for about 2 hours on high.

Let it cool for 5 minutes. Pour the mixture in a blender, and mix until thick but semi-soft. Drizzle with the lemon juice and serve with the toasted pitas.

Crunchy Chicken Curry

Ingredients:

- 4 tbsp of olive oil

- 4 legs of chicken (organic) thighs

- 1 tsp of mustard (dry)

- ½ cup of almond meal

- 1 tsp of cayenne powder

- 1 tsp of curry powder

- Salt and pepper

Instructions:

Separate the thigh and legs by cutting it.

Add the chicken into the crock pot. Season it with pepper and salt. Pour a little amount of olive oil. Cover and cook on high for 2 hours.

Set the oven to 350 degrees fahrenheit.

On a baking plate, mix the mustard, almond meal, cayenne, and curry powder. Roll the chicken and coat them with the mixture. Drizzle with olive oil and roast for an hour or until chicken turned into crispy and crunchy brown.

Roasted Sprouts

You will need:

- Salt and pepper

- 1 lb of Brussels sprouts

- 2 tbsp of lard

Instructions:

Trim the stems of the sprouts and remove the leaves. Cut into half.

Add all the ingredients to the slow cooker. Cook for about 2 hours on low.

Set the oven to 400 degrees Fahrenheit.

In a frying or roasting pan, put some lard and place it inside the oven and let it melt for 2 minutes.

Add the sprouts and slightly toss. Season the mixture with salt and pepper.

Cook on high for 45 minutes until sprouts are fully roasted.

Serve over a bowl of rice!

Walnut And Apple In Creamy Mustard (Slaw)

Ingredients:

- Salt

- ¼ tsp of fresh ground pepper

- ½ cup of chopped walnuts

- 2 tbsp of mayonnaise (your brand)

- 3 cups of cabbage (finely shredded)

- 1 medium red apple (cut into cubes)

- ¼ tsp of Dijon mustard

- 3 tbsp of walnut oil

- 2 tbsp of apple cider vinegar

Instructions:

Turn the oven on to 350 degree Fahrenheit.

In a glass baking tray, grease the pan using the walnut oil and spread the walnuts onto the pan. Preheat for 8-10 minutes.

On the other hand, trim the bottom and top of the apple remove the core and cut it into quarters. Mix it with the cabbage in a medium bowl.

Whisk all of the remaining ingredients and toss lightly to mix.

Remove the pan from the oven and add the walnuts with the bowl of apple.

Mix the mayonnaise or dressing and coat the veggies. Chill for 2 or 3 hours and serve!

Easy Crockpot Breakfast Pie

Ingredients:

- 1 sweet potato-shredded
- 8 medium eggs-whisked
- 1 yellow onion-diced
- 1 lb of pork sausage–organic
- 2 tsp of garlic powder
- Salt and pepper
- 2 tsp of basil-dried

***toppings and garnish could be avocado, squash, pepper and cilantro

Instructions:

Grease the slow cooker with bacon fat or coconut oil.

Put the ingredients into the slow cooker and use a wooden ladle to stir and mix.

Cook on low for 7 hours stirring occasionally.

Serve and slice the cooked pie.

Enjoy a healthy breakfast!

Lamb Cream Curry

Ingredients:

- 1 small onion-roughly chopped
- 1 lb of bone-in lamb shoulder – grass – fed
- fresh grated ginger
- 2 cloves of garlic-minced
- 1/8 cup of coconut vinegar
- 1 can of coconut milk-13 oz
- ¼ tsp of freshly ground pepper
- 1 tsp of salt
- ½ tsp of coriander-powdered
- 1 tsp of curry powder
- ½ tsp of whole mustard seeds
- ½ tsp of cumin-ground
- ¼ tsp of black pepper powder
- ¼ tsp of turmeric-ground
- 1/8 tsp of cinnamon-ground
- 1/8 tsp of cloves-ground

- 1/8 tsp of cayenne pepper

Sprig of fresh cilantro

Bow of cauliflower rice

Instructions:

Cut the meat into chunks. Set aside.

Chop the onion coarsely and the garlic.

Slice the gingers into half.

Combine the ginger, onion, coconut milk and all other ingredients into the crockpot.

Stir and mix well. Add the pieces of lamb chunks.

Gently stir to submerge the lamb meat into the coconut milk mixture.

Cover with the lid on. Set to cook on low for 5 hours.

Stir and serve! (Usually meat will fall off the bone)

Remove the bones and serve over the cauliflower rice.

Garnish it over with the fresh cilantro sprig!

Chili-Beef Verde

Ingredients:

- 1 tsp of cilantro – dried
- 2 cups of beef broth – homemade
- 2 tsp of salt
- 1 tsp of cumin-powdered
- ½ tsp of black pepper
- ¼ cup of olive oil
- ½ tsp of oregano leaves – dried
- ¼ cup olive oil
- 2 pieces of jalapeño –seeded and diced
- ¾ lb of Anaheim chilies –seeded and diced
- 5 cloves of garlic-minced
- 1 ½ lbs of pork tenderloin –grass-fed
- 1 medium onion- diced

Instructions:

Combine the olive oil with the broth and all spices into the slow cooker.

Top it with the pork loin meat.

Cover and cook for 6 hours on low.

Serve and enjoy!

Ginger-Carrot Soup

Ingredients:

- ½ tbsp of chopped onion

- 5 large carrots- coarsely chopped

- 2 cups of chicken broth-homemade

- ½ lime-juiced

- 1 tbsp of curry powder

- ½ tsp of cumin

- 1 medium ginger-peeled and minced

- 5-6 large carrots, chopped

- Salt and pepper

- 1 can of coconut milk-14 oz

Instructions:

It is very basic. Combine all the ingredients except for the coconut milk into the slow cooker. Cook for about 6 hours on low.

Using a blender, puree the mixture until achieves the desired thickness of soup.

Add the coconut milk and blend for another minute.

Enjoy the soup!

Red Curry Soup

Ingredients:

- 1 can of coconut milk -14.5 oz

- 4 cups of turkey broth – organic and homemade

- 2/3 cup of red curry paste

- 1 tbsp of fish sauce

- 4 baby carrots –shredded

- 2 large turnips (or potatoes)

- 1 tbsp of red chili paste or red chili flakes

- 3 cloves of garlic-minced

- 4 cups of turkey meat – organic (cut into bite-size)

- 1 white onion-medium

Instructions:

Put all the ingredients into your slow cooker. Mix using a wooden ladle and stir to combine.

Cover and cook for 8 hours until vegetables are fully cooked.

You can add some spices in your bowl as per your preference.

Bacon-Sprouts In Butter

Ingredients:

- 5 oz of bacon

- 1 lb of Brussels sprouts

- 1 tbsp of Dijon mustard

- Salt and pepper

- 2 tbsp of butter

+ 3-4 tbsp of bacon grease

Instructions:

In a small frying pan, heat butter and cook the bacon on medium-high until bacons are crisp. Let it cool for 5 minutes. Using the back of spoon, crumble the bacon into bits or you can use your bare hands.

Wash and rinse the sprouts. Trim the stems and cut them into half.

Combine all the ingredients into the crock pot. Add the sprouts and bacon bits.

Cook on low for exactly 4 hours and it's about perfect! Serve!

Roasted Walnuts In Honey-Butter

Ingredients:

- 1 tsp of vanilla extract
- 3 tbsp of butter –low fat, unsalted and grass-fed
- ¼ cup of raw honey
- 2 cups of raw walnuts
- ½ tsp of pumpkin pie spice –cloves, ginger, cinnamon and nutmeg

Instructions:

Grease the slow cooker using the butter. Heat until butter melts.

Combine the vanilla, pumpkin spice and honey into the butter and mix well. Add the walnuts and toss to coat the walnuts with the butter mixture.

Cook for about 1 hour on high and keep it covered. Make sure to occasionally stir the slow cooker.

Serve and enjoy!

**if there will are leftovers (which I don't think there will be) put it in an airtight container and refrigerate.

Chicken Tikka Masala

You will need:

- Prepared Cauliflower Rice

- 5 chicken breast (halved, skinless & boneless, cut to 1 inch segments)

- Chopped cilantro

- ½ large yellow onion (finely diced)

- 1 tablespoon of arrowroot powder

- 4 cloves of garlic (minced)

- 1 cup of almond milk (water or coconut milk)

- 2 tablespoon of fresh ginger (finely grated)

- 2 bay leaves

- 1 1/2 can of tomato puree

- 1 red pepper (stemmed, seeded & sliced in half)

- 1 cup of cashew crème

- 1-3 teaspoon of cayenne pepper

- ½ cup of almond milk

- ¾ teaspoon black pepper

- 2 tablespoon of olive oil (extra-virgin)

- ¾ teaspoon of cinnamon powder

- 2 tablespoon of lemon juice

- 2 teaspoon of celtic sea salt

- 2 tablespoon of garam masala

- ½ tablespoon of paprika powder

- 1 tablespoon of ground cumin

Instructions:

To make the cashew cream, put 1 cup of raw cashew nuts in 3 cups of water that has been boiling for 30 minutes and soak it.

Take the cashews and put in a blender together with 1 cup of the liquid from the pot and blend until consistency is smooth.

Put together cayenne pepper, onions, pepper, garlic, cinnamon, ginger, salt, tomato puree, paprika, cashew cream, cumin, ½ cup of almond milk, garam masala, olive oil and lemon juice. Stir all ingredients to combine.

Put half of the portion of the sauce to the slow cooker then put the cubed chicken then pour the remaining sauce over it.

Put 2 bay leaves and red pepper.

Cook for approximately 6 hours on low while the lid is securely on.

After 5 ½ hours, whisk in a separate bowl arrowroot and 1 cup of almond milk and pour it carefully to the slow cooker and gently mix it.

Let it cook for 20 more minutes to give you time to prepare the cauliflower rice.

Take the red pepper and bay leaves before you serve the dish with cauliflower rice. Garnish with cilantro leaves.

White Bean Chili

You will need:

- 1 jalapeño (seeded & diced)
- 4 cups of soaked white beans (24 hours)
- Salt and pepper to taste
- 4 cups of organic vegetable broth (low sodium)
- 1 teaspoon smoked paprika
- 2 medium sized sweet potatoes or yams (peeled & diced)
- 1 teaspoon of chili powder
- 1 bell pepper (diced)
- 1 tablespoon of ground cumin
- 1 small medium yellow onion (diced)
- 5 cloves of garlic (peeled & minced)

Instructions:

Wash and drain the beans well.

Put the beans, garlic, yellow onion, bell pepper, chili powder, jalapeno, vegetable broth, smoke paprika and sweet potatoes or yam into the slow cooker. Blend well.

Cook for at least 4 to 6 hours with the lid securely on.

Chili Pork with Cauliflower Rice

You will need:

- 2 pounds of pork shoulder (pork butt)
- Salt and pepper
- 1/2 onion (chopped)
- 1/4 cup of cilantro (chopped leaves only)
- 2 cans of 4 ounce size of green chilies
- 2 limes (with zest)
- ¼ cup of lime juice
- 1/2 teaspoon of garlic powder
- 1/4 cup of broth (from the slow cooker)
- 1/2 cup of chicken broth
- 1 head of cauliflower (riced)
- 1 tablespoon of chili powder
- Cilantro Lime Rice (Cauliflower)
- 1 teaspoon of garlic powder
- 1/2 teaspoon of cayenne
- 1 teaspoon of salt
- 1 teaspoon of cumin

- 1 teaspoon of pepper

Instructions:

Put into the slow cooker onions and ½ cup of chicken broth.

Put together all the spices in a separate bowl.

Generously rub the spices to the pork roast to coat it well.

Add 2 limes to the slow cooker, two cans of chilies and the pork roast.

Cook for approximately 6 to 8 hours.

As soon as the pork is cooked, work on the cauliflower rice.

Put the chopped head of the cauliflowers to a food processor until the texture is rice-like.

Add the rice-like cauliflower in a pan and add ¼ cup of the broth from the slow cooker then put ½ teaspoon of garlic powder.

Cook the cauliflower for about 10 to 12 minutes with occasional stirring.

As soon as the rice is cooked mix in the zest of 2 limes and juice, salt, pepper and cilantro.

Pulled Pork

You will need:

- 1 tablespoon of pepper

- 4 pound bone in pork shoulder

- 1 full batch of barbeque sauce

- 4 tablespoon of smoked paprika

- 2 teaspoon of cayenne pepper

- 2 tablespoon of sea salt

- 1 tablespoon of ground white pepper

- 2 tablespoon of chili powder

- 1 tablespoon of oregano (dried)

- 2 tablespoon of ground cumin

Instructions:

Put together the barbeque sauce, cumin, oregano, pepper, paprika, cayenne pepper, sea salt, chili powder and white pepper in a bowl and mix well.

Generously rub thoroughly the spice on the meat and cover it tightly with plastic wrap and put inside the refrigerator for a minimum of 3 hours or longer.

When you decided to cook this recipe, unwrap the pork roast and put it in the slow cooker and add ¼ cup of water and cook for about 8 to 10 hours.

Shred the pork and put it back to the slow cooker with barbeque sauce and cook for another 60 minutes on low.

Beefy Chili

You will need:

- 1 cup of celery (diced)

- 2 pounds of ground beef

- 1 can of 15 ounce of tomato sauce

- 1 onion (diced)

- 1 can of 14 ounce of diced tomatoes

- 3 cloves of garlic (minced)

- 1 can of 28 ounce of crushed or stewed tomatoes

- 1 red and 1 green bell pepper (diced)

- 1 jalapeno (minced)

- 1 cup of carrots (minced)

  Spices

- 1 teaspoon of salt

- 3 tablespoons of chili powder

- 1/2 teaspoon of cayenne

- 1 tablespoon of oregano

- 1 teaspoon of onion powder

- 1 tablespoon of basil

- 1 teaspoon of pepper

- 2 tablespoon of cumin

  Garnish

- 1 or 2 avocados (diced)

- 4 pieces of bacon (fried & crumbled)

Instructions:

Cook garlic and onions and saute them in a saucepan.

Put the ground beef and sear it in a pan until browned.

Remove the excess fat.

Put the browned beef and cooked onions to the slow cooker.

Put all the spices and vegetables to the slow cooker and mix it well.

Cook for approximately 6 hours on low.

Put avocado sliced and crumbled bacon to garnish.

Pesto Chicken Salad

You will need:

- Salt and pepper

- 1 ½ pound of chicken breasts (organic & boneless)

- 1/4 teaspoon of garlic powder

- 1 clove of garlic (chopped)

- 1 cup of chicken broth (organic)

- 1/2 white onion (chopped)

  Pesto Sauce

- 1/2 lemon (juiced)

- 1/4 cup of pine nuts

- 1 cup of fresh basil

- Dash of red pepper flakes (optional)

- 1 1/2 cup of spinach

- 1 tablespoon of parmesan cheese (optional)

- Dash ground pepper,

- 1/2 cup of cashews (any preferred nuts)

- Dash of Himalayan sea salt

- 1 tablespoon of olive oil (extra-virgin)

- 1 clove of garlic

Instructions:

Put the chicken, chicken broth, garlic, onion, garlic powder, salt and pepper to the slow cooker and cook for around 6 to 8 hours.

As the chicken is in the slow cooker, prepare the pesto and put inside the refrigerator.

As soon as the chicken is cooked shred it to bite-sized segments and add it to the pesto sauce.

Cashew Chicken

You will need:

- 2 tablespoon of organic ketchup (or tomato paste)

- 1/4 cup of arrowroot starch

- 1/2 cup of raw cashews

- 1/2 teaspoon of black pepper

- 1/4-1/2 red pepper flakes

- 2 pounds of chicken thighs (cut into bite-size segments)

- 1/2 teaspoon of ginger (minced)

- 1 tablespoon of coconut oil

- 2 cloves of garlic (minced)

- 3 tablespoon of coconut aminos

- 1/2-1 tablespoon of palm sugar

- 2 tablespoon of rice wine vinegar

Instructions:

Put black pepper, starch and chicken inside a re-sealable plastic bag. Toss the chicken inside to coat evenly.

Cook chicken in a pan with coconut oil for approximately 5 minutes until it is browned and transfer it in the slow cooker.

Combine red pepper flakes and coconut aminos in a bowl and pour to the chicken inside the slow cooker.

Cook for approximately 3 to 4 hours on low with cover securely in place.

Mix in the cashew to the slow cooker when you are about to serve.

Balsamic Roast Beef

You will need:

- ½ cup balsamic vinegar

- 3 to 4 pounds chuck roast

- Sea salt and pepper

- 1 medium onion (diced)

- A pinch or two of red pepper flakes

- 6 cloves of garlic (minced)

- 2 tablespoons of coconut aminos

- 1 cup chicken or beef stock

Instructions:

Put inside the slow cooker the whole chuck roast with the fat side facing the bottom of the cooker.

Put balsamic vinegar, salt, pepper, onion, red pepper flakes, garlic, coconut aminos and stock on top of the chuck roast.

Cook for approximately 8 hours on low while keeping the lid on.

Take the chuck roast out of the slow cooker and pour the remaining onion, garlic and juices to a food processor or blender until you have your preferred texture for your gravy.

Slice the chuck roast and serve it with gravy.

Italian Beef

You will need:

- 1 teaspoon of dried oregano
- 2 ½ to 3 pounds of beef
- 1 tablespoon of tomato paste
- 2 cups of carrots (chopped)
- 2 cups of beef stock
- 1 small yellow onion (sliced)
- 1 ½ cups of crushed tomatoes (organic)
- 4 to 5 cloves of garlic (chopped)
- A pinch of red chili flakes
- 1 teaspoon of kosher salt
- 1/8 teaspoon of ground cinnamon
- 1 teaspoon of garlic powder
- 1/2 teaspoon of dried thyme
- 1 teaspoon of dried basil

Instructions:

Put the cubed beef inside the slow cooker together with basil, carrots, oregano, onions and garlic. Also add the thyme, red chili flakes, salt, garlic powder and cinnamon.

Pour to the slow cooker the crushed tomatoes and beef stock. Mix in the tomato paste and stir well.

Cook for about 5 to 6 hours on low while the cooker is covered.

You can serve this dish with your favorite pasta.

Breakfast Casserole

You will need:

- 1 cup coconut milk

- 1 pound of chorizo sausage

- Oil or ghee for greasing the crockpot

- 1 small onion

- 1 small butternut squash

- 12 eggs

Instructions:

Cook the chorizo in a pan. When fat is visible put the onions and cook it until they are wilted.

Whisk the coconut milk and eggs.

Remove the seeds, peel and slice the squash.

Use a non-stick cooking spray to coat the slow cooker.

Combine egg and milk mixture, squash and onion and sausage mixture. Mix well and make sure that all the other ingredients are coated by the egg mixture.

Cook for approximately 8 to 10 hours on low and serve.

Smoked Beef Roast

You will need:

Coffee Spice Rub

- ½ tablespoon of garlic powder
- 2 tablespoons of coffee grounds
- 1 teaspoon of sea salt
- ½ teaspoon of ground chipotle
- 1 tablespoon of cumin
- 1 teaspoon of cocoa powder (unsweetened)
- 1 tablespoon of dried oregano
- ¼ teaspoon of cinnamon

Roast

- 1 red onion (halved & sliced)
- ½ tablespoon of coconut oil
- ¾ cup of water
- 2 ½ pound of beef chuck roast

Instructions:

Put together all ingredients under the coffee spice rub in a bowl and mix well.

Heat your pan with coconut oil on medium to high heat. See to it that you r pan is hot before you put the meat.

Generously rub the coffee spice rub to the roast.

Put the roast in the pan and browned it for about 3 to 4 minutes per side.

Put the sliced onions to the slow cooker and once the roast is browned add it to the slow cooker.

Put water and cook for about 7 to 8 on low or 5 to 6 hours on high while it is covered.

Chicken and Okra

You will need:

- 1 ½ teaspoon of dry Italian seasoning
- 4 chicken legs (bone-in)
- ½ cup of leaf parsley (chopped)
- 3/4 teaspoon of kosher salt (divided)
- 3 cups of sliced okra (fresh or frozen)
- ½ teaspoon of pepper (divided)
- 2 bell peppers (cored & sliced)
- 3 teaspoons of canola oil (organic & divided)
- 1/3 cup of green olives (chopped)
- 4 cloves of garlic (minced)
- 1 can of 28 ounce tomatoes (diced)
- 2 large onions (French cut)
- ½ cup of dry red wine

Instructions:

Cut into two the chicken legs.

Take the fat off and put ½ teaspoon of pepper and ½ teaspoon of salt.

Heat oil in a pan on medium to high heat then cook the chicken and sear the chicken until browned for about 2 to 4 minutes on each side.

Put 1 teaspoon of oil in a pan then put pepper, salt, garlic, Italian seasoning and onion. Stir frequently until the vegetables are turning brown for approximately 3 minutes. Put the onion mixture to the cooker.

Pour wine to the pan and let it simmer. Stir through the pan to get the flavor of other ingredients for 1 minute. Add olives and tomatoes and allow it to simmer. Put the tomato mixture on the onions then adding pepper to the slow cooker and keep it covered.

Cook for about 8 hours on low or for 4 hours on high. At the last 30 minute of cooking time, add the okra and continue cooking for another 30 minutes.
Carefully put the chicken to serving bowls and mix in the vegetables.

Garlic Sage Chicken

You will need:

- Half of a lemon

- 1 whole chicken (rinsed & patted dry)

- Paprika, pepper, salt or any of your preferred seasonings

- Sprigs of fresh sage, thyme, rosemary and marjoram

- 4 cloves of garlic

Instructions:

Break the cloves of garlic but do not peel them.

Put the cloves of garlic in the slow cooker and add the chicken over with the breast side facing up.

Put half of the lemon inside the chicken cavity.

Generously season with salt, other seasonings, pepper and paprika the chicken.

Tear the leaves of the herbs and put surround the chicken with it.

Cook for approximately 8 hours on low.

Put the different chicken parts of the chicken on a baking sheet and broil until the skin is crispy for a few minutes.

Serve it right away together with the garlic cloves.

Choco Chicken Mole

You will need:

- ¼ cup of almond butter

- 2 pounds of chicken pieces (skinless)

- Cilantro, jalapeno and avocado (chopped)

- salt and pepper

- 2 tablespoon of ghee

- ½ teaspoon guajillpo chili powder

- 1 medium onion (chopped)

- ½ teaspoon cinnamon

- 4 cloves of garlic (crushed or minced)

- 1 teaspoon cumin

- 6 to 7 whole tomatoes (peeled, seeded & chopped)

- 1 teaspoon sea salt

- 5 dried New Mexico chili peppers (rehydrated & chopped)

- 2 1/2 ounce of 70 % or above dark chocolate

Instructions:

Put pepper and salt over the chicken to season it.

Heat the ghee in a pan on medium heat and sear the chicken until all sides are browned.

Place the chicken into the cooker.

Sauté onion to the same pan until it becomes wilt.

Put garlic in and cook for 1 to 2 more minutes.

Move the sautéed garlic and onion to the slow cooker.

Put the spices, tomatoes, salt, chili peppers, dark chocolate and almond butter to the slow cooker.

Cook for approximately 4 to 6 hours on low or as soon as you can easily remove the meat.

When you are ready to serve add jalapeno, cilantro and avocado on top.

Enchilada Chicken Stew

You will need:

- 1 can of 7 ounce tomato sauce
- 2 pounds of chicken breasts
- Avocado
- 1 yellow onion (chopped)
- Bundle of cilantro
- 1 green bell pepper (chopped)
- Salt and pepper
- 1 can of 4 ounce jalapenos (chopped)
- 2 teaspoons of dried oregano
- 1 can of 4 ounce green chilies (chopped)
- 1 tablespoon of chili powder
- 2 tablespoons of coconut oil
- 1 tablespoon of cumin
- 1 can of 14 ounce tomatoes (diced)
- 3 cloves of garlic (minced)

Instructions:

Put the chicken breasts into the cooker.

Place all of the other ingredients over the chicken.

Cook for about 8 to 10 hours on low or you can set it to high and cook for about 6 to 8 hours.

When it is done cooking allow it to cool a little bit so you can shred it with the rest of the ingredients.

Put avocado and cilantro on top as you serve.

Chicken Curry

You will need:

- 1/2 medium red bell pepper (chopped)
- 1 to 1 ½ pounds of chicken breast (diced & boneless)
- 3 cloves of garlic (minced)
- 2 cans of coconut milk
- 1/4 head of cabbage (chopped)
- 3 tablespoon of red curry paste
- 1/4 head of cauliflower (chopped)
- 1 small yellow onion (diced)
- 1/2 medium green bell pepper (chopped)

Instructions:

Dissolve the curry paste in the mixture of chicken broth and coconut milk and pour it to the slow cooker.

Put the cubed chicken to the slow cooker and mix well.

Add the green pepper, onion and red pepper to the slow cooker.

Add the cauliflower and cabbage to the slow cooker too and mix well then followed by the garlic.

Cook for approximately 4 hours and keep it covered.

Tomato, Basil and Beef Stew

You will need:

- 1 pound of ground beef
- 30 ounces of organic diced tomatoes
- 1/4 cup of basil leaves (chopped)
- 1 cup of canned coconut milk (full fat)
- 1 cup of chicken broth
- 1 tablespoon of coconut oil
- 1 teaspoon of salt
- 1 cup onion (diced)
- 3 cloves of garlic (minced)

Instructions:

Put the coconut milk and the diced tomatoes in a blender and blend until texture is smooth.

Sauté onions in coconut oil in a stockpot until the onions are softened. Put the ground beef and cook until it is browned then removed excess fat.

Add in salt and garlic, then put the coconut milk and tomato mixture with the chicken broth. Let it boil and lower the heat and allow it to simmer for another 10 to 15 minutes.

Add basil leaves and you are ready to serve.

Carnitas Nachos

You will need:

- 1 tablespoon of dried thyme

- 3 ½ pound of pork roast

- 1 cup of chicken broth

- Sea salt and pepper

- 4 bay leaves

- Olive oil

Instructions:

Coat the roast pork by rolling it in salt and pepper.

Sear the roast to evenly brown the roast to all sides so the juices will be intact.

Put in the slow cooker the remaining ingredients and cook for a minimum of 6 hours on low.

You can shred the meat before you eat it.

Beef Ribs with Balsamic Vinegar

You will need:

- ½ cup of balsamic vinegar

- 2 to 3 pounds of beef short ribs (with bones)

- 6 cloves of garlic (mashed)

- 1 tablespoon of coconut oil

- 4 whole dried dates

- 1 can of 15 ounce of tomato sauce

Spice Blend:

- 1 tablespoon of garlic powder

- 2 tablespoon of coarse sea salt

- 1 teaspoon of black pepper

- 1 tablespoon of rosemary (dried)

- 1 tablespoon of paprika

- 1 tablespoon of sage (dried)

- 1 tablespoon of onion powder

Instructions:

Combine together the black pepper, sea salt, paprika, dried rosemary, onion powder, dried sage and garlic powder in a bowl.

Generously rub the spiced to the short ribs.

Sear the ribs to a pan with coconut oil for about 2 to 3 minutes on each side.

Move the ribs to the slow cooker and add mashed garlic, tomato sauce, dried dates and balsamic vinegar.

Cook for approximately 4 to 6 hours on low or as soon as the beef is cooked.

Jambalaya Soup

- 1 pound of large shrimp (raw & deveined)
- 5 cups of chicken stock
- 1/4 cup of hot sauce
- 4 peppers (chopped)
- 3 tablespoon of Cajun Seasoning
- 1 large onion (chopped)
- 2 cups of okra
- 1 large can of tomatoes (organic & diced)
- ½ to 1 head of cauliflower
- 2 cloves of garlic (diced)
- 1 package of spicy Andouille sausage
- 2 bay leaves
- 4 ounce of chicken (diced)

Instructions:

Add the chicken stock, peppers, bay leaves, onions, hot sauce, garlic, Cajun seasoning and chicken in the slow cooker.

Cook for about 6 hours on low.

Add the sausage about 30 minutes before the cooking time is up/

As the sausages are being cooked in the slow cooker, prepare cauliflower rice by using a food processor.

After 10 minutes of the sausages being in the slow cooker, mix in the raw shrimp and the cauliflower rice.

Beef Bone Broth

You will need:

- 2 tablespoon of vinegar (preferably Apple Cider Vinegar)

- 1-2 kilogram of beef soup- bones (grass-fed)

- Salt and pepper to taste

- 4 liters of filtered water

- 3 heaped tablespoon of rosemary leaves (fresh)

- 1 large yellow onion

- 4 bay leaves

In a clean flat surface working, chop the onion in quarters; finely chop the garlic and rosemary. Add everything in the slow cooker.

Add salt and pepper and the bay leaves.

Next would be the soup bones and pour in enough water to about half of the slow cooker or until bones are submerged.

Add the apple cider vinegar.

On a low temp, boil the bone and allow simmering for 20 to 24 hours. This is the exact cooking time for beef bone for soup to completely unleash the bone marrow flavor and its nutrients. It may even soften the bones to crumble. Remove from heat and put it in a cooling rack to completely cool down for about an hour. Refrigerate or chill.

Skim the excess fat layered on the top (the jelly form base); put it in a saucer and set aside (you can use this for your next cooking or frying). Reheat the soup and serve! You may want to add the skimmed fat when reheating the soup. It really tastes good! (Optional)

Turkey Broth

You will need:

- 2 tablespoons of vinegar (apple cider vinegar)

- 1 lb of turkey carcasses (you can use roaster carcasses)

- 5 cloves of minced garlic

- 1 fresh lemon (sliced)

- ¼ cups of ginger (sliced)

- Whole black pepper

- Salt

- Water

Instructions:

Combine all of these ingredients in the slow cooker. Fill with enough water for your broth.

Put on the lid cover and let it cook for 12-24 hours on low.

Remove the foamy particles formed on the top or strain. Let it cool for an hour.

Refrigerate overnight or until chilled.

Scrape off the hardened fat. It will be good if it's only the gelatinous broth that you will serve!

Reheat until the soup is reduced and serve hot! You will probably ask for another bowl!

Moroccan Chicken with Apricot Jam

You will need:

- 3 Tablespoons of Cooking oil (ghee, lard or coconut oil)
- Water
- ½ cup of almond butter
- 1 can of tomato sauce (14 ounce)
- 2 ½ cinnamon sticks
- 1 cup of apricot jam
- 1 tablespoon of grated ginger (fresh)
- 1 small lemon (juiced)
- 1 teaspoon of cumin
- 4 minced cloves of garlic
- 1 teaspoon of salt
- ½ teaspoon of Spanish sweet paprika
- 2 yellow onions (sliced)
- 4 lbs of organic chicken thighs
- 1 tablespoon of minced ginger

Instructions:

In a medium bowl, combine the paprika, tomato sauce, salt, apricot, cumin, ginger and salt. Mix together using a clean spoon, softly toss together to blend, then set aside.

Wash and rinse the chicken. Using paper towels, pat dry the chicken thoroughly.

In a frying pan, over medium heat add 2 tablespoon of oil and cook the chicken for about 4 minutes turning the chicken thighs occasionally, to cook it evenly.

In the same pan, add oil and sauté the minced garlic, garlic and onions until you smell the aroma of the seasoning for 2 minutes or until translucent.

Put the chicken and arrange into the slow cooker and add the sautéed ginger.

Deglaze the pan using water. Scrape the bits using a wooden spoon. Add into the crock pot.

Add the almond butter with the cinnamon and mix together.

Add enough water to submerge the ingredients and meat. And put on the lid cover.

Cook for 6 hours on low heat.

Serve and enjoy the dish!

Green Chili Coco Chicken Soup

You will need:

- 1 cup of coconut cream or you may also use coconut milk

- 2 lbs of chicken breasts or thighs (organic, chopped into cubes ½") bite-sized pieces

- 2-3 tablespoons of white flour

- 6 small carrots, chopped into cubes

- ¼ freshly ground black pepper

- 1 medium-size white onion (diced)

- ½ tsp of coriander (ground)

- 1 cup of green chilies (diced)

- ½ cup of cumin (powdered)

- ¼ cups of homemade chicken broth or stock

- 1 teaspoon of salt

- 1 teaspoon of garlic (minced)

***cilantro for serving or garnish

***lime for serving or garnish

Instructions:

Place the chicken thighs into the crock pot. Add the carrots, black pepper, onion, diced chilies, coriander, chicken stock, salt, and cumin. Stir and mix in together until well combined.

Put on the lid cover and cook on low for 5 to 6 hours.

10 minutes before the set time, pour the coconut milk (if using cream; dissolve it first in a small bowl using cold water) and the coconut flour. Mix and continue to stir until the soup is slightly thickens.

Add salt and taste. Add a little bit more of pepper to taste. (Add as necessary)

Splash a dash of lime juice when about to serve.

If you want it to garnish with cilantro then it will be a perfect delightful dish!

Spicy Cilantro Paleo Chicken

You will need:

- 1 tablespoon of olive or ghee (butter or lard will do so)

- 1 yellow onion (large, 2 cups–diced)

- 2 lbs of chicken thighs (nature-pastured, organic)

- 5 cloves of garlic (large, minced) (around 2 tablespoon)

- 1 chili Serrano pepper (around 1 tablespoon, cut the pepper in half)

- 2 cups of fresh cilantro (chopped)

- 1 tablespoon of fresh ginger (finely diced or chopped)

- ¼ teaspoon of black pepper (ground)

- ½ teaspoon of cumin (powdered)

- ¾ teaspoon of coriander (powdered)

- 1 can of coconut heavy cream or coconut milk

***fresh cilantro and crumbled almonds (for garnish)

Instructions:

In a frying pan, add butter or oil and lightly brown the chicken over medium-low about 2 minutes turning chicken thighs occasionally.

Place the chicken into the crock pot.

Remove the seeds of the Serrano chili (if you want the dish to be more spicy then you may leave half of the seeds or more) Add the chili, garlic, ginger and onion into the crock pot. Chop the cilantro leaves coarsely and add to the slow cooker. Season it with salt and pepper. Mix all together. While stirring, add the coconut milk or cream until you achieve a slightly thick sauce.

Put on the lid and cook on low for 5-6 hours or 3-4 hours on high.

In a bowl of rice, scoop the spicy chicken and serve it with cilantro and crumbled almonds on top!

Paleo Beef Borscht in Maple Syrup

You will need:

- 1 bay leaf

- 1 teaspoon of black pepper

- 1 teaspoon of salt

- 3 large beets (peeled and cut into cubes 1")

- 1 onion (medium, chopped)

- 2 potatoes (cut into cubes)

- 1 ½ teaspoon of fresh dill

- 3 tablespoon of maple syrup

- 1 teaspoon of parsley

- 6 tablespoon of red wine vinegar

- 2 medium carrots (cut into bite-size)

- 1-2 pounds of beef (grass-fed)

- 1 can of tomato paste (16 ounce)

- 4 cloves of minced garlic

- 1 can of diced tomatoes (28 ounce)

- 2 cups of beef broth (home-made)

- 1 medium purple cabbage (shredded) (you may use any variety of cabbage)

***for garnish, you may add yogurt or sour cream

Instructions:

You can sear on the beef meat first in a large pan but this is optional.

Combine the beef meat, diced tomato, beets, carrots, onion and potatoes into the crock pot.

Mix the tomato paste, beef broth, garlic, red wine vinegar, dill, parsley, maple syrup, salt and pepper. Mix and incorporate well. Pour in the mixture into the crock pot.

Put on the lid cover and cook on low for 9 hours or until beef is cook to you desired doneness.

For additional 30 minutes, plop the cabbage in and mix it well into the borscht. Cook it on high.

Serve with optional garnishes!

Spicy Chicken, Summer Squash and Sausage Stew

You will need:

- 1 teaspoon of black pepper
- 1 teaspoon of parsley
- 1 teaspoon of salt
- 1 ½ pounds of chicken thighs (or breast, boneless, organic)
- 1 teaspoon of basil
- 12 ounce of spicy sausages (any brand)
- 1 tablespoon of oregano
- 6 ounce of roasted red and green bell peppers
- 1 can of diced tomato (14.5 ounce)
- 3 cloves of garlic (crushed)
- 1 chopped large zucchini
- 1 large white onion (or shallot)
- 2 cups of small squash (patty pan)

Instructions:

If you do experience heartburn when eating, we then suggest to sauté the onions and garlic first before adding it into the crock pot.

Slice or cut the chicken thighs into bite-size.

Chop the sausages and vegetables. And then add together and mix it up.

Add everything to the crock pot and cover.

Cook on low for 8 hours or until chicken is completely cooked.

Add salt and pepper to taste (if needed).

Serve while hot and enjoy!

Wings on Fire

You will need:

- ¼ teaspoon of black pepper

- 3 pounds of chicken wings, organic (you may combine thighs if you want)

- ½ teaspoon of paprika

- ½ cup of softened butter

- ¾ cup of Frank's Red Hot Sauce (or your preference)

- ¼ cup of organic raw apple cider vinegar

Instructions:

Turn on the oven and set it to BROIL. Around ten minutes or so put the chicken into the oven (using of course a microwaveable container) and let it cook for 5 minutes on each side or until chicken wings turn to brown and crispy!

In a saucepan, over low heat melt the butter. Add vinegar, paprika and black pepper and pour in the hot sauce.

Grease the crock pot using butter. Next, add in the chicken thighs and pour the sauce spreading it all over the chicken thighs to coat.

Cover and let it cook for 2 hours on high to make sure that chicken will not be over cooked. (Occasionally stir)

Remove them in the crock pot and serve warm!

Sweet Potatoes in Orange-Sage with Bacon

You will need:

- 1/8 teaspoon of salt
- 3 large sweet potatoes (cut into cubes)
- 1/4 cup of fresh orange juice
- 1 teaspoon of sage
- 2 tablespoon of honey
- 1/2 teaspoon of thyme
- ¼ cups of butter (cubed)
- 4 bacon strips (crumbled)

Instructions:

Spread butter inside the crock pot.

Mix all the ingredients in your slow cooker except for the bacon. Stir in completely until incorporated. Put the butter on top of your mixture.

Cook on low for 3 hours.

Serve with bacon crumbled and enjoy!

Orange Paleo Chicken

You will need:

- ½ teaspoon of red chili flakes or paste
- 2 pounds of chicken thighs (boneless and skinless)
- ½ teaspoon of rice vinegar
- 5 tablespoons of tomato paste
- ½ cup of fresh ginger (grated)
- 1/8 cup of orange juice
- 2 cloves of garlic (minced)
- 4 tablespoon of coconut aminos (or soy sauce)
- 1 teaspoon of sesame oil
- 3 tablespoon of honey
- 2 tablespoon of arrowroot powder

Instructions:

Wash the chicken and put it into the crock pot.

Combine all together in a bowl all of the ingredients except for the arrowroot. Mix well to incorporate.

Cover with the lid and cook for 8 hours on low.

Set aside the chicken, remove it from the slow cooker. Remove chicken from crock pot and set aside. Dissolve the arrowroot powder into the liquid and mix well. Add back the chicken thighs and let it be cooked for another 15 minutes until the sauce thickens up lightly.

Pour on the sauce, serve and enjoy!

Sweet Potato Shepherd's Pea Pie

You will need:

- A crock pot

- ½ cup of beef broth (home-made)

- ¼ cup of water

- 3 cups of sweet potatoes (medium, mashed)

- 1 pound of lamb meat (nature pastured)

- 1 tablespoon of herbs de provence

- 2 cups of frozen peas and carrots (mixed vegetable pack, thawed)

- 1 medium onion (sliced)

- 3 cloves of minced garlic

Instructions:

In a frying pan , put some oil and sear the meat about 3 minutes each side or until brown over medium-high heat. Add some of the onions, garlic and some of the herbs.

Put the lamb meat into the crock pot and the sautéed seasonings. Stir in to mix well.

(I would go for fresh vegetables instead, like fresh carrots and fresh peas and celery, but it's optional and you should have time to prepare all the peeling and cutting of the veggies)

Pour the beef broth and water into the mixture. Spread the mashed sweet potatoes over the meat using a wooden spoon.

Put on the lid cover and cook for 6 hours on low.

Remove cover and stir. Cook for another 5 minutes and turn on the crock pot to high to thoroughly cook the meat.

Serve and enjoy!

Honey Paleo Sesame Chicken

You will need:

- 1 teaspoon of sesame seeds

- 8 pieces or approximately 2.2 lbs of chicken thighs (organic)

- 2 tablespoons of arrowroot powder

- A pinch of salt

- 1 teaspoon of red chili flakes (or chili paste)

- ½ cup of coconut aminos (or soy sauce)

- A pinch of freshly cracked black pepper

- ¼ cup of tomato paste

- 1 white onion (medium, diced)

- 1 cup of honey

- 4 cloves of minced garlic

Instructions:

Wash the chicken thighs and pat dry using paper towels. Season it with salt and pepper. Place the chicken into the crock pot.

In a large bowl, combine all the ingredients except for the arrowroot powder and sesame seeds. Mix well to blend in. Add the mixture into the crock pot and stir. Dissolve

Cover and cook for 8 hours on low or until chicken is cooked thoroughly. Scoop out some of the liquid from the crock pot, put it in a small bowl and add the arrowroot powder and sesame seeds. Stir in to dissolve completely. Pour in the arrowroot mixture back into the crock pot. Cover and cook for another 15 minutes on high temp.

When soup is already creamy thick then you can already serve and eat!

You may want to serve it over with broccoli or steamed cauliflower. Either way you will find it very delicious!

Mongolian Beef Steak

You will need:

- ¼ teaspoon of ground pepper

- 2 pounds of round beef steak (flank steak will do so long as the meat is grass-fed)

- 2 teaspoon of sesame oil

- Around ½ cup of arrowroot powder (or cornstarch for substitute)

- 2 teaspoon of wine vinegar

- ¼ cup of beef broth (homemade)

- 2 small carrots (julienned or bite-size)

- 6 small green onions (chopped)

- 4 cloves of minced garlic

- ½ cup of soy sauce or aminos (gluten-free)

- 2 teaspoon of ginger (freshly grated)

- 1 tablespoon of chili paste (or red chili flakes)

- 1 teaspoon of molasses

- 2 tablespoon of honey

- 1 tablespoon of low-fat butter

***sliced scallions and steamed broccoli for garnish (optional)

Instructions:

Slice the meat into thin strips.

In a medium bowl, put the arrowroot powder and dredge the steak strip until fully coated. Set aside.

Put all the remaining ingredients into the slow cooker and combine well until incorporated.

Mix the coated meat. Toss slightly to combine it with the mixed ingredients.

Cover and cook for 6 hours on low or until meat is cooked to desired doneness.

Smoked Ham with Apples and Spinach

You will need:

- 1 can of frozen spinach, thawed (16 ounce)
- 5 pounds of smoked ham (pork shoulder, grass-fed)
- 2 cups of water (or more as needed)
- 2 big red apples (diced) (you may use Granny Smith apples)
- 2 cups of dry white wine
- A pinch of red pepper flakes
- 2 turnips (large, peeled and cut into bite-size)
- A pinch of coriander (ground)
- 5 sprigs of fresh parsley
- 1 bay leaf
- 2 cloves of diced garlic
- 4 tablespoon of garlic

Instructions:

Trim or remove the bottom pits of the apple so it may sit on the bottom of the slow cooker. Add the turnips and ham on top. Except for the spinach, add the remaining ingredients, except for the spinach and add the wine then the water.

Put the cover on and cook for 8 hours on low.

Carefully remove the ham from the crock pot and put in a bowl. Let sit for at least an hour.

Add the spinach and mix well. Put the ham on top of the mixed ingredients and cook for 30 minutes more on high.

Using a slotted spoon, remove the apples, spinach and turnips.

Put one apple on a plate; arrange the portions on each side of the turnips and ham.

Sweet Moroccan Beef Brisket

You will need:

- 2 tablespoon of honey

- 2 pounds of beef brisket (boneless, nature fed or grass-fed)

- ½ cup of beef broth (homemade is best)

- 1 medium red onion (quartered)

- 1 cup of dry red wine

- 2 medium parsnips (julienned)

- 1 cup of dried apricots (6 ounce package)

- 1 teaspoon of black pepper (freshly ground)

- 2 cloves of large garlic (minced or crushed)

- ¼ teaspoon of salt

- ¼ teaspoon of powdered nutmeg

- 2 teaspoon of powdered coriander

- 2 teaspoon of powdered cinnamon

- 2 teaspoon of powdered cumin

***fresh cilantro leaves for serving

Instructions:

Place the onions and parsnips into the slow cooker.

In a small bowl, incorporate the garlic, pepper, nutmeg, salt, cinnamon, coriander and cumin. Using your bare hand, rub in the mixture onto the beef brisket evenly and put the meat on top of parsnips and onion.

Pour in the beef broth, red wine and honey. Lightly stir in the ingredients together.

Put on the lid cover and cook on low for 8 hours or 6 hours on high.

Serve with the cilantro and rice!

Made in the USA
Middletown, DE
15 December 2015